ACE Mathematics Games 4

13 exciting blackline activities to engage ages 8—9

David Smith

TarquinGroup
www.tarquingroup.com

Acknowledgements

Thanks are due to many people but especially to my lovely wife and also my dear mum who between them patiently played all the games with me to test their initial suitability. I also have to thank the teachers and children of Peel Park Primary School for giving them a road test, spotting my errors and making suggestions on how they could be further developed and improved. Finally thanks go to the staff at Tarquin, for their support in the editing process.

Dedication

This book is dedicated to the memory of Maxine Firth, an inspirational friend and colleague who shared my ideal of an enjoyment of mathematics for all.

Published by Tarquin Publications
Suite 74, 17 Holywell Hill
St Albans
AL1 1DT

www.tarquingroup.com

Distributed in the USA by IPG Books
www.ipgbook.com
www.amazon.com & major retailers

Distributed in Australia by OLM www.lat-olm.com.au

Copyright © David Smith, 2014
ISBN: 978-1-907-55088-1

All rights reserved. Sheets may be copied singly for use by the purchaser only, or for class use under a valid school or institutional licence from the relevant Copyright Licensing society.

Introduction

'By the end of year 4, pupils should have memorised their multiplication tables up to and including the 12 multiplication table and show precision and fluency in their work (mental methods).'

Key Stage 2 National Curriculum Programme of Study

'The teacher created a positive climate for learning in which pupils were interested and engaged.'

OFSTED Inspector

Welcome to a world of mathematical fun and games!

Easy to play and requiring only basic equipment, these educational games engage even the most reluctant of learners whilst boosting confidence for all.

Great for teachers, intervention workers, teaching assistants, private tutors and parents, the flexible nature of this game pack offers:

▶ practice for specific objectives from the new National Curriculum

▶ a great resource to:
   "ensure students are engaged in learning and generate high levels of commitment to learning"
   (Outstanding Grade Descriptors, *Ofsted School Inspection Handbook* (updated 2014))

▶ the opportunity to demonstrate a commitment to:
   "the social development of pupils at the school" within curriculum time
   (Ofsted Framework for School Inspection (updated 2014))

▶ an effective assessment tool

▶ the promotion of problem solving and thinking skills through game strategy

▶ fun homework activities

Playing Information

All these games require a pack of playing cards and most also need some kind of coloured counters or other objects such as beads or buttons. Suitable materials are available from Tarquin - see page 40 for details. When the picture cards are used the jack represents number eleven, the queen is number twelve and the king is thirteen. To help children remember this you may want to consider writing the actual numbers in the corners of each card.

And that's all you need to know to enjoy years of happy gaming!

David Smith

Hexums

Focus

Hexums is a game for two or three players which practices recall of facts for the 6, 7 and 9 multiplication tables.

What you need

▶ Playing cards (kings removed)

▶ Counters (a different colour for each player)

▶ Hexums game board

How to play

When the kings have been removed from the pack the remaining cards are shuffled and placed in a pile, face-down and within reach of all the players. Player 1 turns over a playing card from the pack and places it face-up in front of them. The number on the card is then multiplied: by six if playing Hexums 6, by seven in Hexums 7, and by nine in Hexums 9.

For example (Hexums 6)

Player 1 turns over a four so must say 4 x 6 = 24. After saying the correct answer Player 1 can place a counter on any of the matching answers on the game board.

Player 2 then turns over a card and multiplies the number by six. This time a queen is turned over so Player 2 says 12 x 6 = 72 and can also place a counter on any of the matching answers on the game board.

Players continue to take cards in turn, multiply the number on the card and place their counters on the board. If a player gives an incorrect answer they are not able to place a counter on that turn.

How to win

Each player has to try and make a continuous line of coloured counters on adjacent numbers from the outer ring to the inner ring of shaded hexagons, as shown in the diagram.

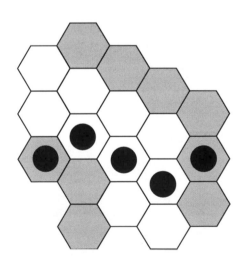

Rule changes / Next steps

▶ Limit the players to twelve counters each to try and get a winner.

▶ Record multiplication facts on paper or a whiteboard. At the end of the game use these to generate other multiplication and division facts (as below) and then test each other.

| 4 x 6 = 24 | so | 24 = 6 x 4 | 24 ÷ 6 = 4 | 6 = 24 ÷ 4 |
| 12 x 6 = 72 | so | 72 = 6 x 12 | 72 ÷ 6 = 12 | 6 = 72 ÷ 12 |

Instruction Sheet © Tarquin Photocopiable under licence – for terms see page 2

Hexums

x 6

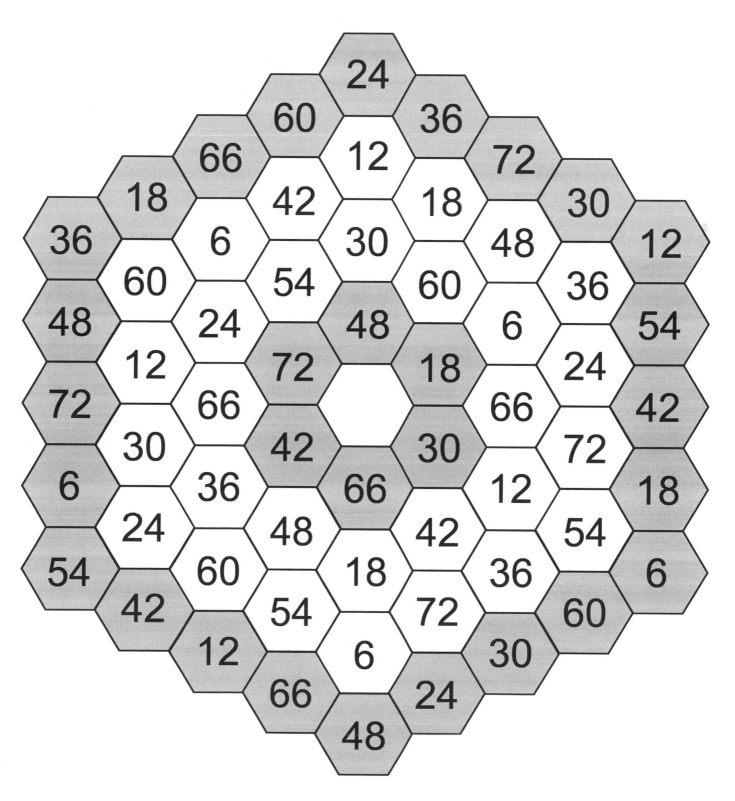

Hexums
x 7

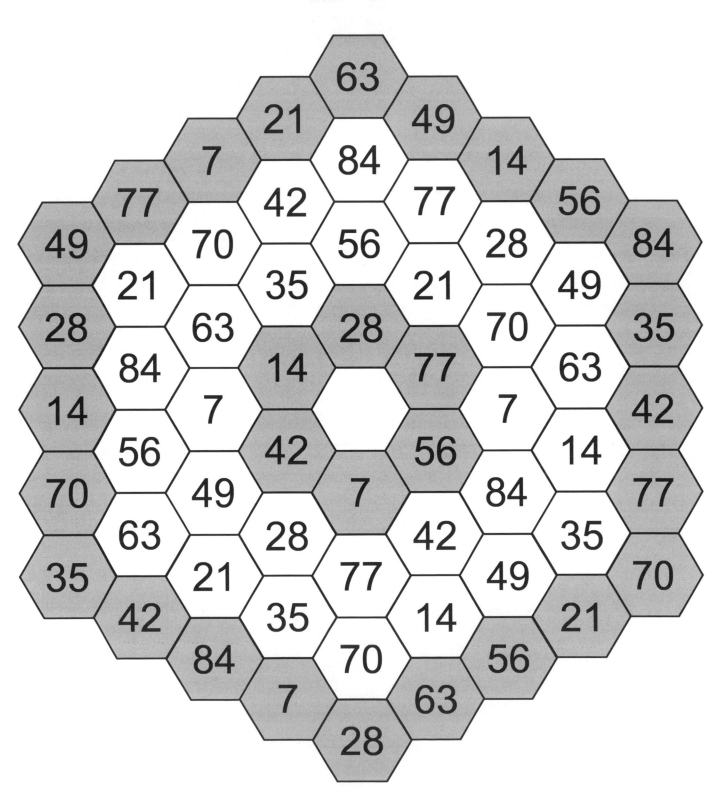

Game Board © Tarquin Photocopiable under licence – for terms see page 2

Hexums
x 9

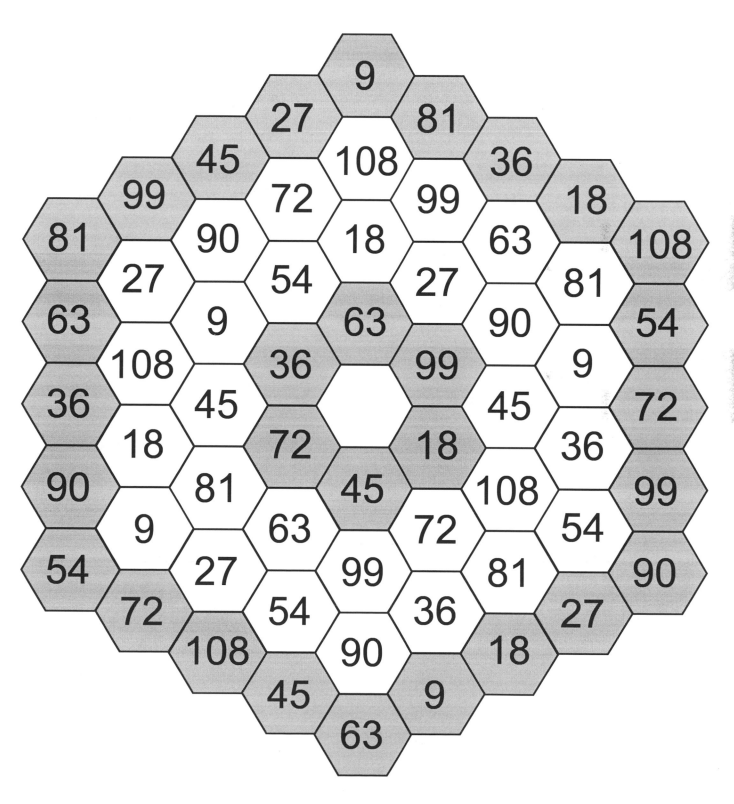

Game Board © Tarquin Photocopiable under licence – for terms see page 2

Square Up

Focus

Square Up is a game for two to four players which practices recall of multiplication facts for the 6, 7 and 9 multiplication tables.

What you need

▶ Playing cards (kings removed)

▶ Counters (a different colour for each player)

▶ Square Up game board

How to play

When the kings have been removed from the pack the remaining cards are shuffled and placed in a pile, face-down and within reach of all the players. Player 1 turns over a playing card from the pack and places it face-up in front of them. The card is then multiplied: by six if playing Square Up 6, by seven in Square Up 7, and by nine in Square Up 9.

For example (Square Up 7)

Player 1 turns over an eight so must say 8 x 7 = 56. After saying the correct answer Player 1 can place a counter on any of the matching answers on the game board.

Player 2 then turns over a card and multiplies the number by seven. This time a jack is turned over so Player 2 says 11 x 7 = 77 and can also place a counter on any of the matching answers on the game board.

Players continue to take cards in turn, multiply the number on the card and place their counters on the board. If a player gives an incorrect answer they are not able to place a counter on that turn. A player may turn over another card if no matching answer can be found on the game board.

How to win

Players have to make the shape of a square, by placing counters on each corner, as shown in the diagram. The square can be any size and the first player to complete one is the winner.

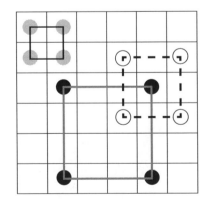

Rule changes / Next steps

▶ Players score four points for each square they make and play can continue until all their counters have been used or until there are no spaces left on the game board.

▶ Make some flashcards showing the multiplication or division facts on one side and the answer on the other side. Children can then use them for individual practice or to test a partner.

SQUARE UP 6

42	36	66	60	24	72
48	72	18	12	36	6
12	30	6	24	54	42
54	60	48	66	30	18
72	18	36	42	12	66
30	24	54	6	60	48

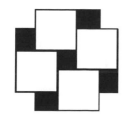
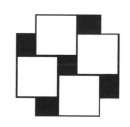

Game Board © Tarquin Photocopiable under licence – for terms see page 2

SQUARE UP 7

49	28	63	84	42	56
14	42	77	70	21	28
35	7	56	49	84	77
84	21	28	63	35	14
56	70	14	42	7	21
7	63	49	77	70	35

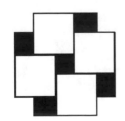

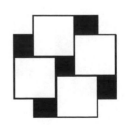

SQUARE UP 9

54	18	72	36	90	108
108	81	99	45	18	9
9	72	27	63	54	81
90	99	36	108	27	45
27	63	54	90	9	72
45	81	18	99	63	36

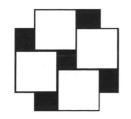 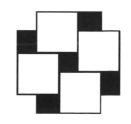

Game Board © Tarquin Photocopiable under licence – for terms see page 2

Total Tables

Focus

Total Tables is a game for two or more players which practices recall of multiplication facts up to 12 x 12.

What you need

▶ Playing cards (tens and picture cards removed)

▶ Counters (a different colour for each player)

▶ Total Tables game board

▶ Total Tables scorecard

How to play

The tens and picture cards are removed from the pack. The remaining cards are shuffled and Player 1 deals three cards to each player, placing the rest of the pack face-down within reach of all the players. Players must multiply two of their cards together, and then have the extra option of either adding or subtracting the value of the third card.

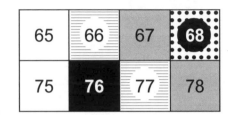

For example

If Player 1 turns over an eight, a seven and a four, the following calculations are possible:

8 x 4 = 32	8 x 4 + 7 = 39	8 x 4 – 7 = 25	8 x 7 = 56
4 x 7 = 28	4 x 7 + 8 = 36	4 x 7 – 8 = 20	8 x 7 – 4 = 52

Placing a counter on total thirty-six scores six points for a grey square, whereas placing a counter on twenty-eight scores twelve points for a striped square. Placing a counter on total thirty-two, however, is not a good idea as it is a dotty square and results in nine points being taken off the player's score.

The player places their cards down, states their calculation and, if correct, places their counter on the relevant square. They then draw three new cards ready for their next turn.

Play goes to the next player and the process is repeated, with players trying to achieve the maximum number of points possible on each turn. Each player keeps their own score using a scorecard. Players must do all their mental calculations before placing their counter and must also give a correct answer in order to do so.

Players cannot place a counter on a square that is already covered and must be ready to put their cards down when it comes to their turn. Players must place a counter unless all possible squares are covered, in which case the player cannot place a counter but draws three new cards as usual. When all the cards have been used, shuffle them and place them in a pile, face down in the middle of the table, ready for the next player's turn.

How to win

The winner of the game is the player with the most points after an agreed number of rounds.

Rule changes / Next steps

▶ Allow players to multiply the numbers on all three cards, such as 2 x 3 x 6 = 36.

▶ Include the picture cards to produce some more difficult calculations, or remove the aces so that there is no multiplying by one.

Instruction Sheet © Tarquin Photocopiable under licence – for terms see page 2

Total Tables

1	2	3	4	5	6	7	8	9	
11	12	13	14	15	16	17	18	19	T
21	22	23	24	25	26	27	28	29	A
31	32	33	34	35	36	37	38	39	B
41	42	43	44	45	46	47	48	49	L
51	52	53	54	55	56	57	58	59	E
61	62	63	64	65	66	67	68	69	S
71	72	73	74	75	76	77	78	79	
81	82	83	84	85	86	87	88	89	
		T	O	T	A	L			100

Full colour game board and scorecards downloadable from www.tarquingroup.com.

Game Board © Tarquin Photocopiable under licence – for terms see page 2

Total Tables Scorecard

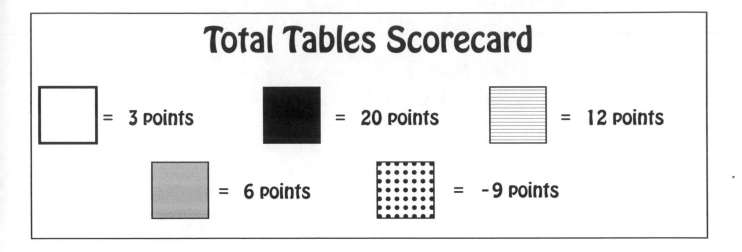

☐ = 3 points ⬛ = 20 points ▤ = 12 points

⬜ = 6 points ⬚ = -9 points

Keep your score like this:

Round Number	Points for square	Total Game points
1	stripes, 12 points	12
2	dotty, -9	12 - 9 = 3
3	grey, 6	3 + 6 = 9

Round Number	Points for square	Total Game points
1		
2		
3		
4		
5		
6		
7		
8		
9		
10		
11		
12		
13		
14		
15		

Multiple Madness

Focus

Multiple Madness is a game for two or more players which practices recognising factor pairs in numbers up to 60.

What you need

▶ Playing cards

▶ Counter

▶ Multiple Madness game board

▶ Whiteboard / paper and pen

▶ Calculator

How to play

The cards are shuffled and placed in a pile, face-down and within reach of all the players. Place a counter on the number thirty position in the middle of the game board. Player 1 takes a card from the top of the pack and can then move the counter the same number of places on the board by either adding or subtracting from thirty.

For example

Player 1 picks a three so they can move the counter to position twenty-seven or thirty-three. Twenty-seven is a multiple of nine so scores nine points, whereas thirty-three is a multiple of eleven so scores eleven points. Therefore, Player 1 decides to move the counter to thirty-three on the game board and starts their scoring with eleven points.

Play passes to the next player and the procedure is repeated.

Players can earn points for multiples from two up to twelve but must claim their points and explain how they know the number they have landed on is actually a multiple of that number. For example, fifty-four is a multiple of two (2 points) but the player could show that it is a multiple of nine (9 points). They can do this by saying things like 9 x 6 = 54, 54 ÷ 9 = 6 or even count up in multiples of nine to show that there really are six lots of nine in fifty-four. Their opponent can challenge an explanation and use a calculator to check whether it is correct.

Players keep a running total of their points using a whiteboard or paper and pen. This may be done by someone acting as a scorer and game referee, who also decides whether player explanations are good enough to award the points.

How to win

The first player to reach a total of sixty points is the winner.

Rule changes / Next steps

▶ Remove the lower value cards from the pack to ensure more practice of mental calculations that require players to add or subtract across multiples of ten.

▶ Allow points for multiples up to fifteen, such as thirty-nine being a multiple of thirteen as 3 x 13 = 39 or sixty being a multiple of fifteen as 4 x 15 = 60. The winning total could then be raised to one hundred points.

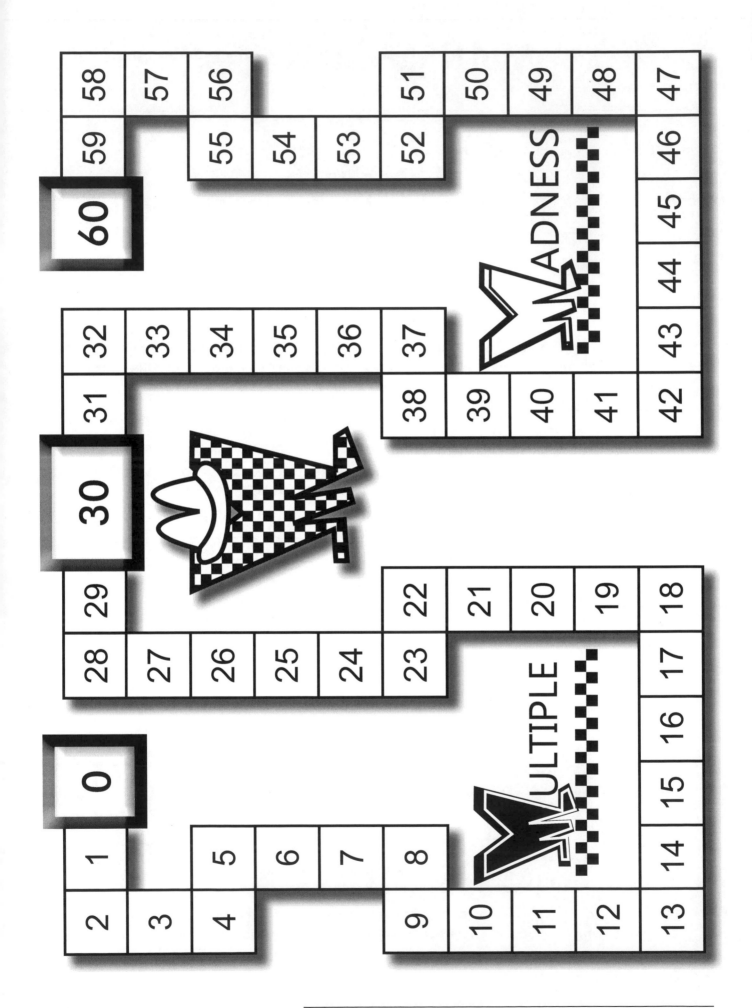

Dare!

Focus

Dare is a game for two or more players which practices counting backwards through zero to include negative numbers.

What you need

▶ Playing cards

▶ Counters (a different colour for each player)

▶ Dare! game board

How to play

Firstly, the cards are shuffled and placed in a pile, face-down and within reach of all the players. Each player places their counter on square 25, which is the starting square. Player 1 takes a card and then subtracts this number from twenty-five, moving their counter to the relevant number on the game board.

Player 1 must then decide whether to play safe, stop and pass the cards to the next player or to 'dare' and turn over another card. If Player 1 decides to dare and turn over another card then:

▶ if the card is the same colour they can continue by subtracting the value of the card from the number underneath their counter;

▶ if the card is a different colour they must go back to the first grey **DARE SQUARE** they reach by moving backwards along the game board.

If Player 1 decides to stop then play goes to Player 2. Play continues with players taking cards in turn and subtracting the value of the card from the number underneath their counter on the game board.

Players are encouraged to do all their mental calculations before moving the counter, but when crossing zero and with negative numbers players may be allowed to count the squares as they move. The player must also give a correct answer to move their counter otherwise it remains in the same place on the game board.

If a player lands on top of another counter, the counter landed on is moved back to the start or the first **DARE SQUARE** they reach by moving backwards along the game board (whichever is agreed by the players before play).

How to win

The first player to land on or go past - 25 (the finish line) on the game board is the winner.

Rule changes / Next steps

▶ Play as a counting up or adding game, starting at -25 and moving up to the finish line.

▶ Each player starts with a blue dare counter and is allowed to use it once at any time during the game. The dare counter forces another player to dare and carry on even when they have decided to stop. The dared player *must* then carry on for two more cards. The same rules apply as outlined previously. However, if they turn over a card of a different colour they must go back to the first **DARE SQUARE** they reach by moving backwards from where they started that turn.

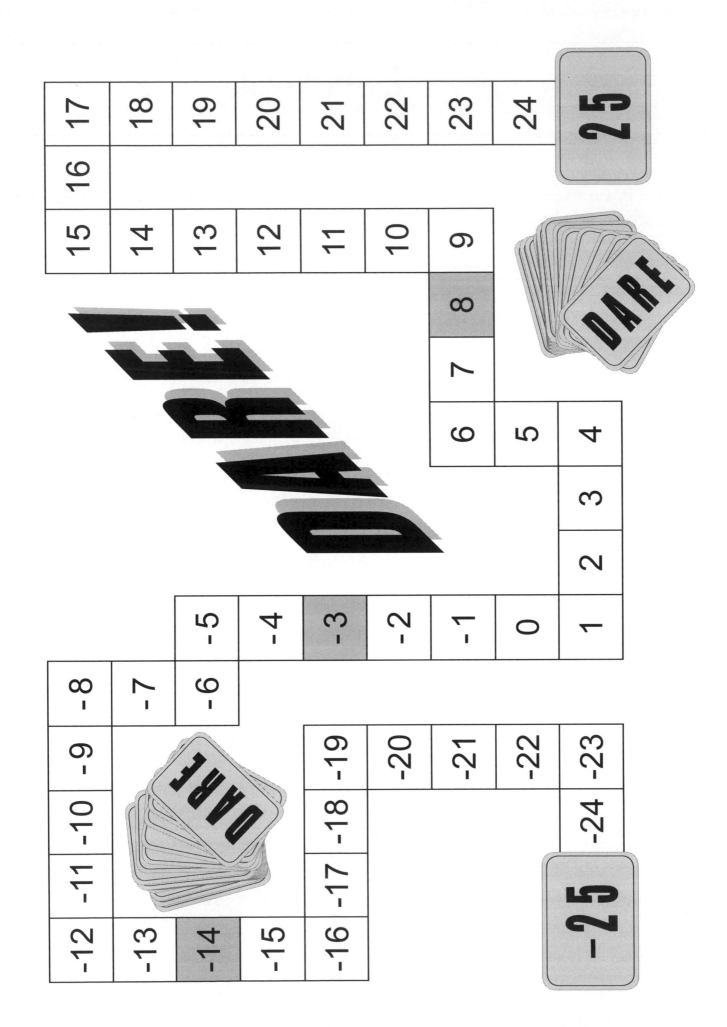

DARE!

Robot Wars

Focus

Robot Wars is a game for two or more players which practices rounding numbers to the nearest 10, 100 and 1000.

What you need

▶ Playing cards (picture cards removed)

▶ Counters (a different colour for each player)

▶ Robot Wars game board

How to play

Player 1 turns over two cards and can then put them together to make a two-digit number. They then write this number in one of the squares on the game board. So if Player 1 turns over a five and a nine they can write fifty-nine or ninety-five. Player 1 decides to write ninety-five.

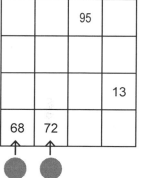

 Player 2 then turns over two cards, a six and an eight. They need to try and make a number that rounds to the same multiple of ten as a number on the board. Sixty-eight rounds to seventy and eighty-six rounds to ninety. Therefore, either one of these numbers has to be written on another empty square on the board, as to be written next to another number, the number must round to the same multiple of ten.

Player 3 then turns over two cards, a three and an ace. Again Player 3 is unable to make a number (thirteen or thirty-one) that rounds to the same multiple of ten as another number on the board so their chosen number has to be written on another empty square. Numbers that do not round to the same multiple of ten cannot be written in an adjacent square unless it is the only option left on the board.

The next player turns over a seven and a two. Twenty-seven doesn't round to the same multiple of ten as any other number on the board so this player decides to make seventy-two as it rounds to seventy, the same multiple of ten as sixty-eight. Both numbers are then covered with coloured counters. As this player was able to place counters they get another turn.

Players continue to take cards in turn and write their numbers on the board, trying to make a number that will round to the same nearest ten as another number already written so they can cover them with counters of their own colour. When all the cards have been used, mix them up and place them back down in a pile within reach of all the players. Play continues until all the squares on the board have been used.

How to win

The winner is the player with the most counters on the game board.

Rule changes / Next steps

▶ Players take three cards and write three-digit numbers, trying to make a number that rounds to the same nearest hundred. Four cards can be taken for four-digit numbers rounding to the same nearest thousand but the cards need frequent collections unless you put two packs together.

Instruction Sheet © Tarquin Photocopiable under licence – for terms see page 2

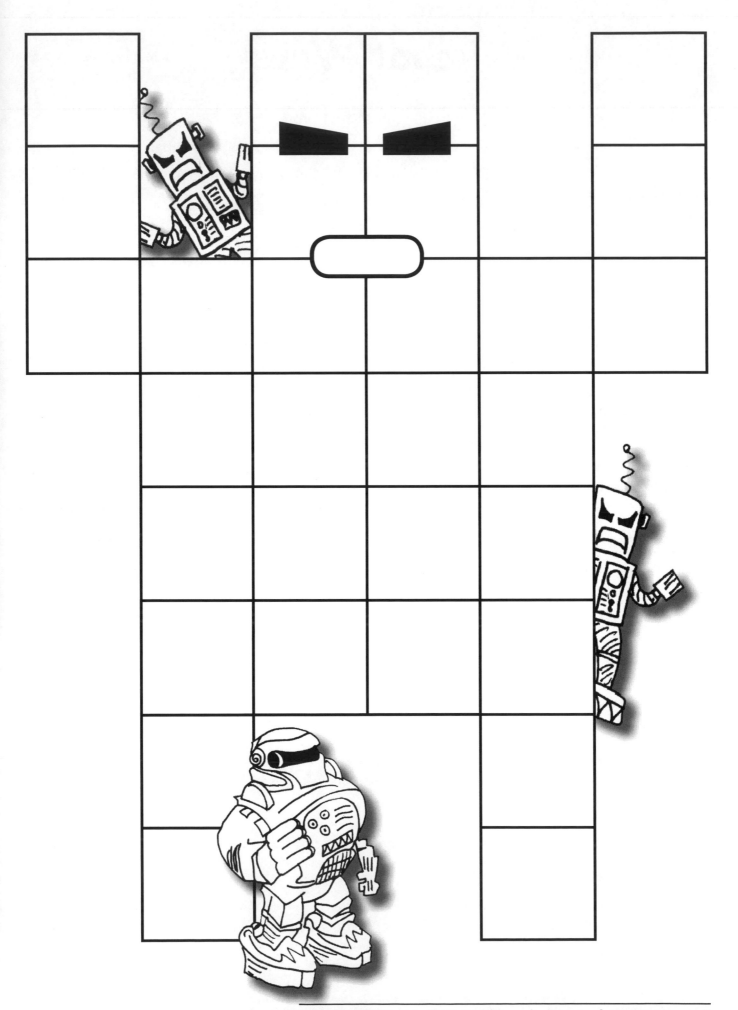

Hooked!

Focus

Hooked! is a game for two players which practices adding and subtracting one and two-digit numbers up to and exceeding one hundred.

What you need

▶ Playing cards (eights and above removed)

▶ Counter

▶ Hooked! game board

How to play

When the higher value cards have been removed from the pack, the remaining cards are shuffled and placed in a pile, face-down between both players. Decide who is counting forwards and who is counting backwards. The player counting forwards moves from left to right along the game board and the player counting backwards moves from right to left. Place a counter on the middle number of the game board.

Players take it in turns to turn over two cards and multiply them together. The total is then added to or subtracted from (depending on the player's direction of play) the number underneath the counter.

For example

Player 1 (adding) turns over a six and a four. They say 6 x 4 = 24, then they calculate 50 + 24 = 74 and move to that square on the game board. Player 2 (subtracting) then turns over a seven and a two. They say 7 x 2 = 14, then they calculate 74 – 14 = 60 and move the counter to that square.

Players must perform the mental calculation before moving the counter, and a correct answer must be given in order to move. When all the cards have been used, shuffle them and place them back down in a pile so that play can continue.

How to win

Player 2 (subtracting) hooks the fish and wins by getting the counter to land on or go past zero whilst Player 1 (adding) hooks the fish and wins by getting the counter to land on or go past one hundred (or one hundred and forty if playing Hooked! 140).

Rule changes / Next steps

▶ Change roles and play again so both players practice their addition and subtraction skills.

▶ Play for a set number of turns and the player who is closest to their end of the game board wins.

▶ For Hooked! 140 include the eights from the pack as well. Players still turn over two cards and multiply them together before adding / subtracting the total to the number underneath the counter.

▶ Encourage children to investigate patterns in adding and subtracting numbers, such as
57 + 24 = 81   67 + 24 = 91   77 + 24 = 101   so   87 + 24 = ____   and so on.

Game Board © Tarquin Photocopiable under licence – for terms see page 2

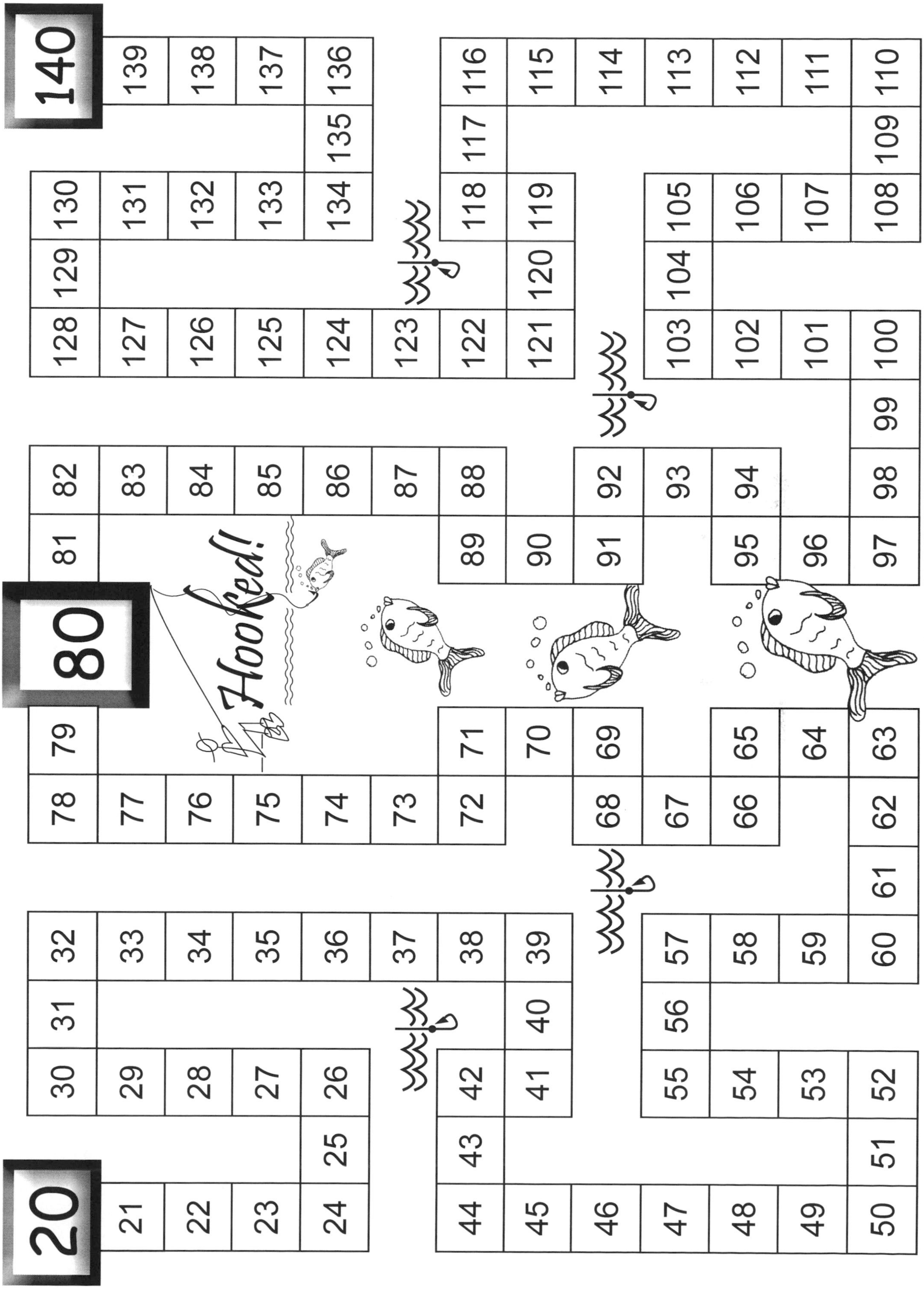

140

139 138 137 136 135

130 129 128 127 126 125 124 123 122 121 120 119 118 117 116 115 114 113 112 111 110

134 133 132 131

109 108

107 106 105 104 103 102 101 100

99 98 97

82 83 84 85 86 87 88

81

89 90 91 92 93 94 95 96

80

Hooked!

79 78 77 76 75 74 73 72 71 70 69 68 67 66 65 64 63

62 61 60 59 58 57

32 33 34 35 36 37 38 39

31 30 29 28 27 26

40 41 42 43 44 45 46 47 48 49 50

55 56 54 53 52 51

20

21 22 23 24 25

Speed Seekers

Focus

Speed Seekers is a game for two or more players which practices adding and subtracting one and two-digit numbers up to and exceeding one hundred.

What you need

▶ Playing cards (aces to fours removed)

▶ Counters (a different colour for each player)

▶ Speed Seekers game board

How to play

Firstly, the cards are shuffled and then placed in a pile, face-down and within reach of all the players. Player 1 takes a card from the top of the pack and doubles its value to get a total. They then subtract this total from one hundred and move their counter on the board as shown in the diagram.

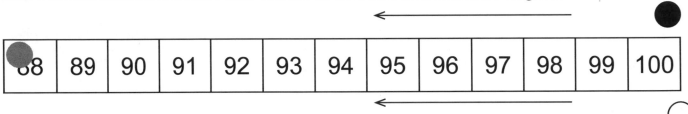

For example

Player 1 (grey counter) turns over a six. First of all they calculate double six (or 2 x 6 = 12). They then calculate 100 − 12 = 88 and move their counter to that position on the game board.

Play goes to Player 2, and play continues with players taking cards in turn, doubling them and then subtracting the total from the number underneath their counter on the game board.

▶ Players must do all their mental calculations before moving their counter. The player must also give the correct answer to move their counter otherwise it remains where it is on the game board.

▶ If a player lands on a Speed Seeker (grey) square they can choose to either move another nine spaces or move any one other player backwards nine squares on the game board.

▶ If a player lands on top of another counter, the counter landed on is moved back to the first Speed Seeker square they reach by moving backwards along the game board.

How to win

The first player to land on or go past zero (the finish line) on the game board is the winner.

Rule changes / Next steps

▶ For Speed Seekers 160 the fours can be put back in the pack and the card turned over is multiplied by three before subtracting that amount from the number underneath the player's counter. Players landing on a Speed Seeker square can choose to either move forward nineteen spaces or move any other player back nineteen squares on the game board.

▶ Play as an addition game, starting at the lower number and adding up to the finish line.

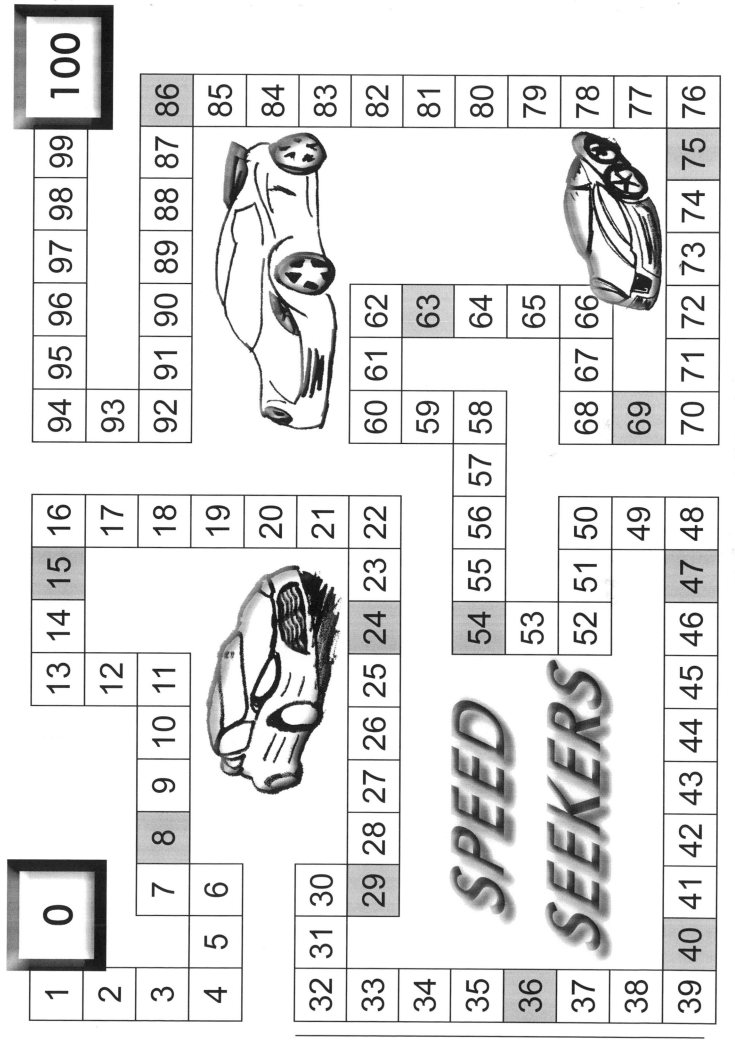

Speed Seekers

40

160

41 42 43 44 45 46 47 48 49 50 51 52 53 54 55 56 57 58 59 60 61 62 63 64 65 66 67 68 69 70 71 72 73 74 75 76 77 78 79 80 81 82 83 84 85 86 87 88 89 90 91 92 93 94 95 96 97 98 99 100 101 102 103 104 105 106 107 108 109 110 111 112 113 114 115 116 117 118 119 120 121 122 123 124 125 126 127 128 129 130 131 132 133 134 135 136 137 138 139 140 141 142 143 144 145 146 147 148 149 150 151 152 153 154 155 156 157 158 159

Double Double Cross

Focus

Double Double Cross is a game for two or three players which practices doubling and halving two-digit numbers with some answers exceeding 100.

What you need

▶ Playing cards (tens and picture cards removed)

▶ Double Double Cross game board

▶ Coloured pencil crayons / felt tips

▶ How to play

When the tens and picture cards have been removed from the pack the remaining cards are shuffled and placed in a pile, face-down between both players. Player 1 begins by turning two cards from the top of the pack and placing them face-up to make a two-digit number. They must then double or halve the number they have chosen.

For example

Player 1 turns over the following cards and can then use them to make any two-digit number calculation such as those below.

Double 68 = 136   Halve 68 = 34
Double 86 = 172   Halve 86 = 43

Player 2 checks the calculation and if correct Player 1 can mark the position of that number on the number line with a coloured cross. Player 2 then takes two cards, a five and a three as shown here. Only whole numbers can be marked with a cross so Player 2 has to double fifty-three or thirty-five and mark the position of that answer on the number line.

Double 35 = 70
Double 53 = 106

Play continues with players taking two cards, doubling or halving the number they make, and marking the answers on the number line.

How to win

The first player to get four crosses of their own colour together in a line wins the game. The numbers do not need to be consecutive but must not be separated by a cross of the opponent's colour, as shown in the diagram.

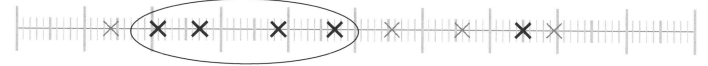

Rule changes / Next steps

▶ Remove the aces and twos to make larger numbers.

▶ Play on the hundred number line and allow players to halve odd numbers and mark their position with a cross (larger doubles can't be marked).

▶ Make links:
double 68 = 136 **so** double 680 = 1360;
halving 68 = 34 **so** halving 680 = 340.

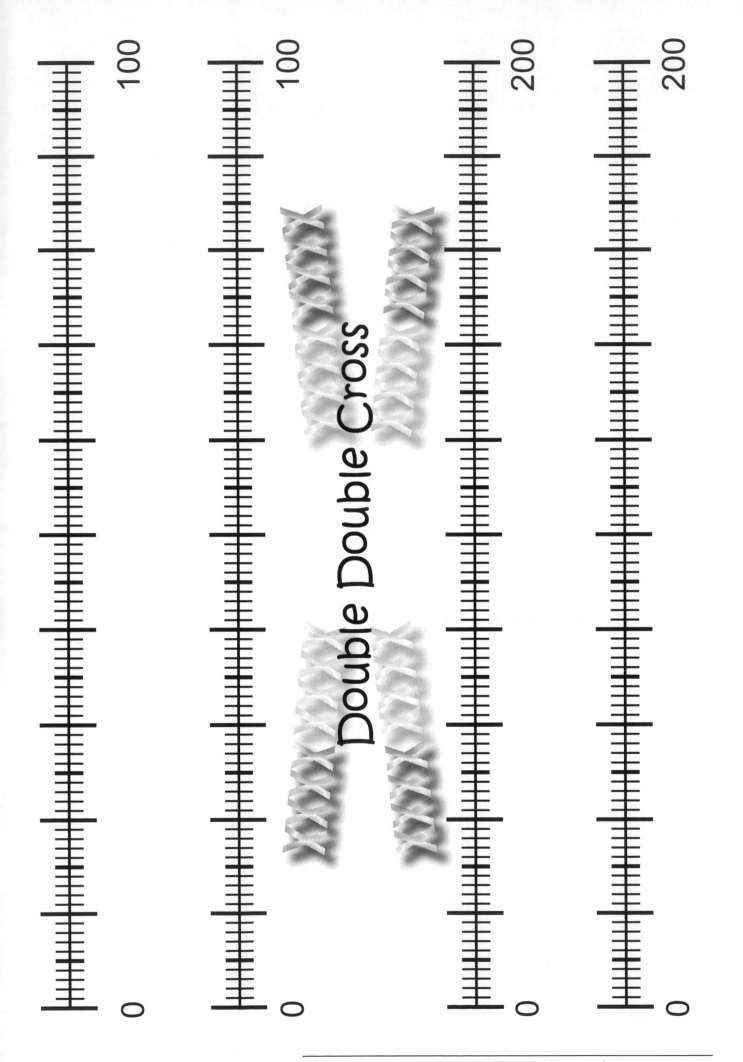

Double Double Cross

Battle Squares

Focus

Battle Squares is a game for two or more players which practices multiplying by ten and adding and subtracting three-digit numbers up to one thousand.

What you need

▶ Playing cards (tens and picture cards removed)

▶ Counters (a different colour for each player)

▶ Battle Squares game board

▶ Battle Squares scorecard

How to play

When the tens and picture cards have been removed from the pack the remaining cards are shuffled and placed in a pile, face-down and within reach of all the players.

Player 1 turns over two cards and uses them to make a two-digit number which they then multiply by ten.

For example

If Player 1 turns over a 3 and a 7 they can either make the number 370 or 730. They must then calculate how much more needs to be added to each number to make one thousand, whilst thinking about how many points they will get for placing a counter on a particular colour.

Player 1 may decide to calculate 370 + 630 = 1000 and put a counter on 630 to score fifty points for a black square. However, if Player 1 decided to calculate 730 + 270 = 1000 and put a counter on 270, they would score one hundred points for a grey square.

Play continues with players taking it in turns to make two-digit numbers, multiply them by ten, and calculate how many more to make one thousand. They then decide where to place their counters on the board to score the maximum number of points possible (players should watch out for dotty squares, which lose them points). Each player keeps their own score using a scorecard. Players must do all their mental calculations before placing their counter and must also give a correct answer in order to do so.

If a square is already covered by a counter then the player must switch their cards around to make the other two-digit number and must place their counter on the other available square. If both possible squares are covered then the player cannot place a counter but draws two new cards on their next turn. When all the cards have been used, shuffle them and place them in a pile, face-down, ready for the next player's turn.

How to win

The winner of the battle is the player with the most points after an agreed number of rounds.

Rule changes / Next steps

▶ Do calculations as subtraction from one thousand, such as 1000 − 540 = 460 or 1000 − 450 = 550.

▶ Players turn over three cards and can use any combination of them to make a two-digit number before multiplying by ten.

▶ Play "in colour" : a full colour downloadable game board and scorecards are available on our website, www.tarquingroup.com.

Instruction Sheet © Tarquin Photocopiable under licence – for terms see page 2

BATTLE SQUARES

10	20	30	40	50	60	70	80	90	
110	120	130	140	150	160	170	180	190	S
210	220	230	240	250	260	270	280	290	Q
310	320	330	340	350	360	370	380	390	U
410	420	430	440	450	460	470	480	490	A
510	520	530	540	550	560	570	580	590	R
610	620	630	640	650	660	670	680	690	E
710	720	730	740	750	760	770	780	790	S
810	820	830	840	850	860	870	880	890	
	B	A	T	T	L	E			1000

Game Board © Tarquin Photocopiable under licence – for terms see page 2

BATTLE SQUARES SCORECARD

= 20 points   = 50 points   = 200 points

= 100 points   = -90 points

Keep your score like this:

Round Number	Points for square	Total Game points
1	stripes, 200 points	200
2	dotty, -90	200 - 90 = 110
3	grey, 100	110 + 100 = 210

Round Number	Points for square	Total Game points
1		
2		
3		
4		
5		
6		
7		
8		
9		
10		
11		
12		
13		
14		
15		

End of the Line

Focus

End of the Line is a game for two to four players which can be used to practice a range of efficient mental methods with numbers up to sixty.

What you need

▶ Playing cards

▶ Counters (a different colour for each player)

▶ End of the Line game board

▶ Whiteboard / paper and pen

How to play

Player 1 turns over two cards from the top of the pack and places them next to each other. They must then look to see if they can make a multiple of two, three, four, or five (depending on which track on the game board is being played) by adding, subtracting multiplying or even dividing the numbers on the cards.

For example (using game board track 1: multiples of two up to 24)

Player 1 turns over an eight and a five as shown. Player 1 is not able to make a multiple of two that appears on the line, so play passes to Player 2, who turns over another card and tries to make a multiple of two using any or all three of the numbers on the cards.

With a three, Player 2 can now make a multiple of two in many different ways:

$5 + 3 = 8$ $8 + 5 + 3 = 16$ $8 \times 3 = 24$ $5 - 3 = 2$ $8 - 5 + 3 = 6$ $8 + 5 - 3 = 10$

Player 2 decides to remove the eight and the three from the line and covers the matching multiple of twenty-four on the top row of the game board with a counter of their colour.

Player 3 then turns over another card and places it next to the five to see if they can make a multiple of two. Player 3 turns over a ten and decides they can make a multiple of two by calculating $10 \div 5 = 2$. They remove the ten and the five and place a counter on the matching number on the top row of the game board.

The next player turns over two new cards and starts the line again. Play continues with players taking it in turns to place cards in the line and attempting to make multiples of two that have not been covered by a counter. A time limit can be set for players to make a multiple and if they can't do it in that time the next player has their turn.

How to win

The winner is the player with the most counters on the line when the last multiple is covered.

Rule changes / Next steps

▶ Play the game using any of the different sets of multiples on the game board or have a go at playing two different sets of multiples at the same time.

▶ Allow players to put cards together to make a two-digit number, such as a three and a four to make thirty-four or forty-three.

Instruction Sheet © Tarquin Photocopiable under licence – for terms see page 2

| 2 | 4 | 6 | 8 | 10 | 12 | 14 | 16 | 18 | 20 | 22 | 24 |

| 3 | 6 | 9 | 12 | 15 | 18 | 21 | 24 | 27 | 30 | 33 | 36 |

END of the LINE

| 4 | 8 | 12 | 16 | 20 | 24 | 28 | 32 | 36 | 40 | 44 | 48 |

| 5 | 10 | 15 | 20 | 25 | 30 | 35 | 40 | 45 | 50 | 55 | 60 |

Game Board © Tarquin Photocopiable under licence – for terms see page 2

Trios

Focus

Trios is a game for four to six players which can be used to practice a range of efficient mental methods with numbers up to one thousand.

What you need

▶ Playing cards

▶ Counters (a different colour for each player)

▶ Trio game board

How to play

Player 1 turns over any number of cards and may be asked to add, subtract or multiply them to get an answer depending on what skill or knowledge from the Year 4 programme of study the game is being used to practice. If the player gets the answer correct they can place a counter of their own colour in a circle on the game board.

Player 2 then turns over one or more cards and performs a similar calculation. Play continues in this way with players taking it in turns to take one or more cards, answer questions and place counters on the game board. If a player gives an incorrect answer, they are unable to place a counter on that turn.

How to win

The first player to make a Trio is the winner. Trios can either be in a triangle or in a straight line as shown in the diagram. Triangles formed can be small or large but the corners must be joined by lines on the game board.

Remove all the counters and play again.

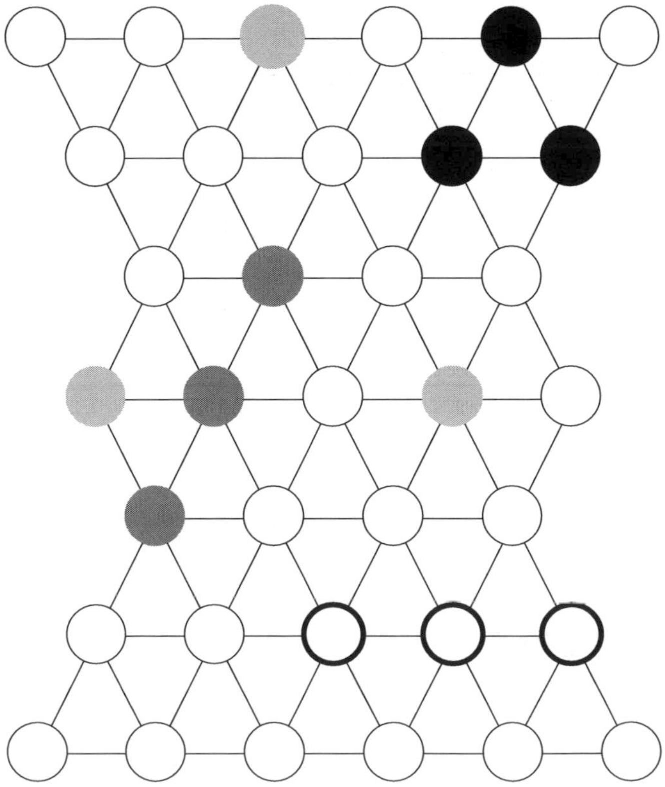

Rule changes / Next steps

▶ Players continue to try and make Trios until all the spaces are covered or until the players agree that no more can be made. Players score three points for every Trio they make and the winner is the player with the most points at the end of the game.

▶ Restrict players to making only triangles or straight lines to win the game rather than allowing both.

TRIOS

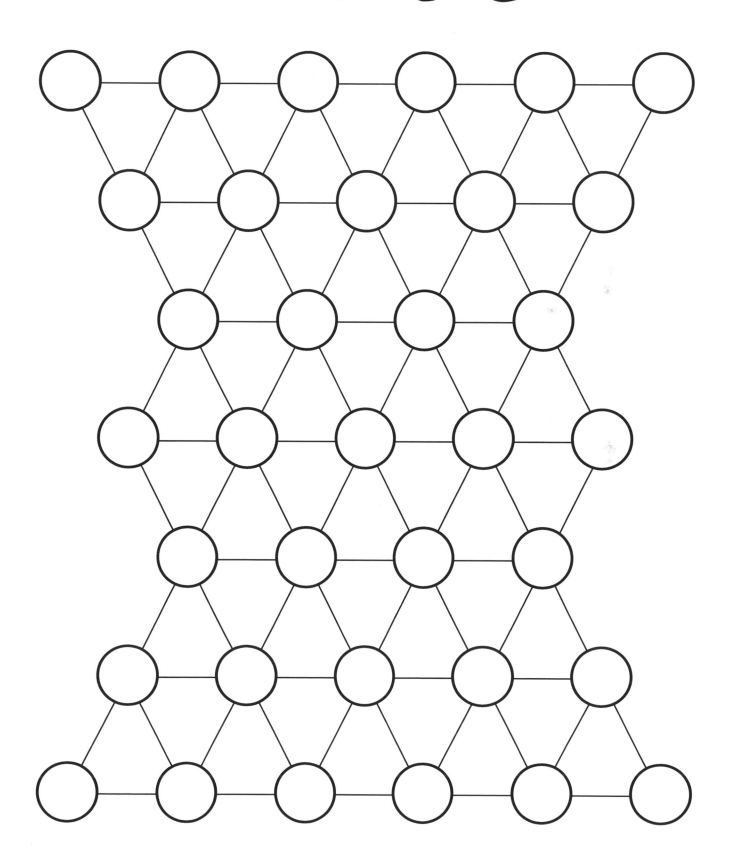

Game Board © Tarquin Photocopiable under licence – for terms see page 2

Monster Mash-Up

Focus

Monster Mash-up is a game for two to six players which can be used to practice a range of efficient mental methods with numbers up to ten thousand.

What you need

▶ Playing cards (cards 1–5)

▶ Counters (one for each player)

▶ Monster Mash-Up game board

▶ Question cards, if using (see Next Steps, below)

How to play

When the cards from six upwards have been removed from the pack the remaining cards are shuffled and placed in a pile, face-down and within reach of all the players. Players then choose a monster and place their counter on it, ready for the start of the game.

Player 1 is asked a question by the question master to practice recall of facts or any skill within the Year 4 programme of study. If answered correctly Player 1 turns over a card and can then move the same number of spaces on the game board. If the answer is incorrect the player is not allowed to move their counter. The other players are then asked questions in turn. If correct they can turn over a card and move the same number of spaces on the game board.

 Players must try and avoid the black holes in various positions on the game board, since landing on one sends them back to 'their' monster at the start of the game.

Players are allowed to move between tracks and go anywhere on the board, though can't keep moving backwards and forwards from one square to another.

If a player lands on top of another counter, the counter landed on is moved back to any monster of that player's choosing.

How to win

The first player to land on or go beyond an end square is the winner.

Rule changes / Next steps

▶ Players can move one bonus square if they can answer a question that another player has answered incorrectly.

▶ Different kinds of question may be selected, dependent, for example, on what a particular child needs to practice, or on particular skills needed for assessment purposes.

▶ Players must turn the exact number to land on an end square and win the game.

▶ Use the set of mixed mental questions provided. Put them face-down on the table for children to pick at random, read aloud and then answer. Alternatively, pass them to an appointed question master to read out.

Instruction Sheet © Tarquin Photocopiable under licence – for terms see page 2

Game Board © Tarquin Photocopiable under licence – for terms see page 2

What two numbers come next? 18, 24, 30, 36, … , …	What two numbers come next? 84, 77, 70, 63, … , …	What is 9 more than 99?	What is 25 less than 200?
What is 1000 more than 8601?	What is 1000 less than 1058?	What is the 6 worth in 7068?	What is the value of the underlined digit in 5483?
True or False 1366 > 3045	True or False 8008 < 7999	Write the number six thousand one hundred and seven in figures.	Write the number three thousand and ninety in figures.
2481 = 2000 + 300 + ___	9146 = 8000 + _____ + 46	Take six tens away from 5400.	Take four hundreds away from 9000.
What is 357 rounded to the nearest 100?	What is 95 rounded to the nearest 10?	XXXVI =	LIX =
3700 + 400 =	6003 – 800 =	760 + 170 =	640 – 160
68 + 75	112 – 84	87 = __ + 29	45 = 62 – __
__ + 300 = 2100	__ – 200 = 4000	What is the sum of 68 and 53?	What is the difference between 78 and 113?

3 x 9 =	7 x 8 =	12 x 6 =	6 x 9 =
8 x 11 =	6 x 7 =	63 ÷ 7 =	48 ÷ 6 =
How many lots of 9 are there in 108?	How many groups of 7 can you make from 49?	If 7 x 12 = 84, what is 7 x 120?	If 9 x 9 = 81, what is 90 x 9?
66 = __ x 6	__ ÷ 9 = 5	8 = 56 ÷ __	6 x __ = 36
What is one sixth of 24?	What is one ninth of 72?	One quarter of a number is 7. What is the number?	I think of a number and find one fifth. The answer is 11. What is the number?
True or False ⅓ > ¼	True or False 0.6 < ½	What is the decimal equivalent of ¼?	What is the fraction equivalent of 0.75?
What is ⅛ of 40?	What is ⅓ of 36?	What is ⅞ - ⅜?	What is two sevenths and four sevenths?
What two numbers come next? 0, 0.1, 0.2, 0.3, … , …	What two numbers come next? 1.1, 1, 0.9, 0.8, … , …	Name another fraction which is equivalent to ½. Explain how you know.	How many thirds are there in four whole ones?

Tarquin Mathematics Resources

Tarquin has more than a thousand product lines to support and enrich mathematics. You can browse them at **www.tarquingroup.com**.

To make it easy to buy what you need to really use this book, we have some special packages online — put the keyword ACE into the quick search box to see the full range at once.

▶ Packs of Playing Cards

▶ Coloured Counters

▶ Beads

Other Tarquin Products designed for you

Books

First Tables Colouring Book

Second Tables Colouring Book

Arithmetic Arithmetic

Tables Cubes

Mathematical Vocabulary 2

The Week's Problem

A Puzzle a Day

Junior Mathematical Team Games

Junior Mini Mathematical Murder Mysteries

Posters

One Million Poster

Multiples Poster

Equal Parts Poster

Quadrilaterals and Polygons Poster

Roman Numerals Poster

Dice and other Manipulatives

Excellent prices on 12-sided and 10-sided dice classroom packs — ideal for mental mathematics.

Tarquin, Suite 74, 17 Holywell Hill, St Albans, AL1 1DT
Tel: +44 (0)1727833866 Fax: +44 (0)845 456 6385
www.tarquingroup.com   Follow us on Twitter @TarquinGroup